THROUGH OUR EYES

Poems and Pictures about Growing Up

POEMS SELECTED BY

Lee Bennett Hopkins

PHOTOGRAPHS BY

Jeffrey Dunn

Little, Brown and Company

Boston Toronto London

To Maria Modugno

Who saw —

Who sees.

Copyright © 1992 by Lee Bennett Hopkins
Photographs copyright © 1992 by Jeffrey Dunn

First Edition

Copyright acknowledgments appear on page 32

Library of Congress Cataloging-in-Publication Data

Through our eyes : poems and pictures about growing up / poems selected
    by Lee Bennett Hopkins ; photographs by Jeffrey Dunn. — 1st ed.
        p.   cm.
    Summary: Color photographs and poems by such writers as Langston
    Hughes and Jack Prelutsky depict children from diverse backgrounds
    engaged in contemporary activities and thoughts.
    ISBN 0-316-19654-1
    1. Children's poetry, American.   [1. American poetry —
    Collections.]   I. Hopkins, Lee Bennett.   II. Dunn, Jeffrey, 1953–
    ill.
    PS586.3.T56   1992
    811'.540809282 — dc20   91-13875

10 9 8 7 6 5 4 3 2 1

SC

Published simultaneously in Canada
by Little, Brown & Company (Canada) Limited

Printed in Hong Kong

Contents

Poem for Rodney   5
Nikki Giovanni

City Blockades   6
Lee Bennett Hopkins

This Is My Rock   7
David McCord

Who Am I?   9
Felice Holman

The New Kid on the Block   11
Jack Prelutsky

Beginning on Paper   13
Ruth Krauss

Song of Frustration   15
Lois Duncan

Lisa   17
Beverly McLoughland

Father   19
Myra Cohn Livingston

My Key   21
Elizabeth Smith

Hope   22
Langston Hughes

Star I Wish On   23
Sandra Liatsos

On Halloween   25
Aileen Fisher

December   27
Sanderson Vanderbilt

I Ask My Mother to Sing   29
Li-Young Lee

To Dark Eyes Dreaming   31
Zilpha Keatley Snyder

Poem for Rodney

Nikki Giovanni

people always ask what
am i going to be
when i grow
up and i always
just think
i'd like to grow
up

City Blockades

Lee Bennett Hopkins

I feel so small
standing beneath the tall
buildings that wall
me and the pigeons in
from the light of the
sky.

This Is My Rock

David McCord

This is my rock,
And here I run
To steal the secret of the sun;

This is my rock,
And here come I
Before the night has swept the sky;

This is my rock,
This is the place
I meet the evening face to face.

Who Am I?

Felice Holman

The trees ask me,
And the sky,
And the sea asks me
    Who am I?

The grass asks me,
And the sand,
And the rocks ask me
    Who I am?

The wind tells me
At nightfall,
And the rain tells me
    Someone small.

    Someone small
    Someone small
    But a piece
        of
          it
        all.

The New Kid on the Block

Jack Prelutsky

There's a new kid on the block,
and boy, that kid is tough,
that new kid punches hard,
that new kid plays real rough,
that new kid's big and strong,
with muscles everywhere,
that new kid tweaked my arm,
that new kid pulled my hair.

That new kid likes to fight,
and picks on all the guys,
that new kid scares me some,
(that new kid's twice my size),
that new kid stomped my toes,
that new kid swiped my ball,
that new kid's really bad,
I don't care for her at all.

Beginning on Paper

Ruth Krauss

on paper
I write it
on rain

I write it
on stones
on my boots

on trees
I write it
on the air

on the city
how pretty
I write my name.

Song of Frustration

Lois Duncan

I have a sister who writes on walls
And rides her tricycle through the halls
And drowns her dolls in the bathroom sink
And takes the last of the orange drink
And sucks her thumb and screams at bugs
And hides her sandwiches under the rugs
And rips my books and won't take naps
And always sits on the company's laps.

I have a sister who's almost four.
Sometimes I wish that she lived next door.

Lisa

Beverly McLoughland

Lisa's father is
Black
And her mother is
White,
And her skin is a
Cinnamon
Delight,
Her hair is
Dark
And her eyes are
Light,
And Lisa is
Lisa,
Day and
Night.

And Lisa is
Lisa,
Night and
Day,
Though there are
People
Who sometimes
Say —
Well, is Lisa

That,
Or is Lisa
This? —
Lisa is
Everything
She is.

Lisa is
Lisa,
Day and
Night,
And her skin is a
Cinnamon
Delight,
And Lisa is
Sun
And Lisa is
Star,
And Lisa is
All
The dreams that
Are.

Father

Myra Cohn Livingston

I look for you on every street,
wondering if we'll ever meet.

In every crowd I try to see
your face. I think you'd know it's me.

I watch our corner where the bus
stops, hoping you'll come back to us.

Mom says I'd better just forget
about you. But I haven't yet.

My Key

Elizabeth Smith

I don't go to day care
Or a sitter anymore.
Now that I am grown up
I've a key to my front door.

I check my pocket through the day,
Making sure I have my key.
I call my mom when I get home
To tell her all is right with me.

I get a little scared sometimes
When there's no one else at home.
The TV keeps me company —
I'm not all that alone.

I like the grown-up feeling
Of having my own key.
But every now and then I wish
My mom was home with me.

Hope

Langston Hughes

Sometimes when I'm lonely,
Don't know why,
Keep thinkin' I won't be lonely
By and by.

Star I Wish On

Sandra Liatsos

Star I wish on,
star above,
send me parents
I can love.
Send me a house
with my own little room.
Send me away
from loneliness —
gloom.

On Halloween

Aileen Fisher

We mask our faces
and wear strange hats
and moan like witches
and screech like cats
and jump like goblins
and thump like elves
and almost manage
to scare *ourselves.*

December

Sanderson Vanderbilt

A little boy stood on the corner
And shoveled bits of dirty, soggy snow
Into the sewer —
With a jagged piece of tin.

He was helping spring come.

I Ask My Mother to Sing

Li-Young Lee

She begins, and my grandmother joins her.
Mother and daughter sing like young girls.
If my father were alive, he would play
his accordion and sway like a boat.

I've never been in Peking, or the Summer Palace,
nor stood on the great Stone Boat to watch
the rain begin on Kuen Ming Lake, the picnickers
running away in the grass.

But I love to hear it sung;
how the waterlilies fill with rain until
they overturn, spilling water into water,
then rock back, and fill with more.

Both women have begun to cry.
But neither stops her song.

To Dark Eyes Dreaming

Zilpha Keatley Snyder

Dreams go fast and far
  these days.
They go by rocket thrust.
They go arrayed
  in lights
    or in the dust of stars.
Dreams, these days,
  go fast and far.
Dreams are young, these days,
  or very old,
They can be black
  or blue or gold.
They need no special charts,
  nor any fuel.
It seems, only one rule applies,
  to all our dreams —
They will not fly except in open sky.
  A fenced-in dream
    will die.

Thanks are due to the following for the works reprinted herein:

BOA Editions Ltd. for "I Ask My Mother to Sing" from *Rose* by Li-Young Lee. Copyright © 1986 by Li-Young Lee. By permission of BOA Editions Ltd., 92 Park Avenue, Brockport, NY 11420.

Curtis Brown Ltd. for "City Blockades" by Lee Bennett Hopkins. Copyright © 1972 by Lee Bennett Hopkins. Reprinted with permission of Curtis Brown Ltd.

Farrar, Straus & Giroux, Inc. for "Poem for Rodney" from *Spin a Soft Black Song* by Nikki Giovanni. Copyright © 1971, 1985 by Nikki Giovanni. Reprinted by permission of Farrar, Straus & Giroux, Inc.

HarperCollins Publishers for "On Halloween" from *Out in the Dark and Daylight* by Aileen Fisher. Text copyright © 1980 by Aileen Fisher. Illustrations copyright © 1980 by Gail Owens. Reprinted by permission of HarperCollins Publishers.

Felice Holman for "Who Am I?" from *At the Top of My Voice*. (Charles Scribner's Sons, 1970). By permission of the author.

Alfred A. Knopf, Inc. for "Hope" from *Selected Poems of Langston Hughes*. Copyright 1942 by Alfred A. Knopf, Inc.; renewed 1970 by Arna Bontemps and George Houston Bass. Reprinted by permission of the publisher.

Ruth Krauss for "Beginning on Paper." Used by permission of the author, who controls all rights.

Sandra Liatsos for "Star I Wish On." Used by permission of the author, who controls all rights.

Little, Brown and Company for "This Is My Rock" from *One at a Time* by David McCord. Copyright 1929 by David McCord. First appeared in the *Saturday Review*. Reprinted by permission of Little, Brown and Company.

Beverly McLoughland for "Lisa." Used by permission of the author, who controls all rights.

Macmillan Publishing Company for "Father" from *There Was a Place and Other Poems* by Myra Cohn Livingston. Copyright © 1988 by Myra Cohn Livingston. Reprinted with permission of Margaret K. McElderry Books, an imprint of Macmillan Publishing Company.

William Morrow and Company for "The New Kid on the Block" from *The New Kid on the Block* by Jack Prelutsky. Copyright © 1984 by Jack Prelutsky. Used by permission of William Morrow and Company.

Elizabeth Smith for "My Key." Used by permission of the author, who controls all rights.

Zilpha Keatley Snyder for "To Dark Eyes Dreaming" from *Today Is Saturday*. (Atheneum, 1969). Copyright © 1969 by Zilpha Keatley Snyder.

Westminster Press for "Song of Frustration" from *From Spring to Spring* by Lois Duncan. Copyright © 1982 by Lois Duncan. Reprinted by permission of Westminster Press/John Knox Press.